Piano • Vocal

Art Songs for Children

13 Songs for the Young Classical Voice

To access companion recorded accompaniments online, visit:
www.halleonard.com/mylibrary

1879-0487-4771-7582

ISBN 978-1-4950-8566-6

HAL•LEONARD®

7777 W. BLUEMOUND RD. P.O. BOX 13819 MILWAUKEE, WI 53213

In Australia Contact:
Hal Leonard Australia Pty. Ltd.
4 Lentara Court
Cheltenham, Victoria, 3192 Australia
Email: ausadmin@halleonard.com.au

Visit Hal Leonard Online at
www.halleonard.com

Other Song Collections for Children, with online accompaniments

The Boy's Changing Voice
20 Vocal Solos
00121394

Christmas Solos for Kids
00740130

25 Folksong Solos for Children
00154679

36 Solos for Young Singers
00740143

36 More Solos for Young Singers
00230109

Contents

Pianists on the recordings: [1] Brendan Fox, [2] Richard Walters, [3] Laura Ward

ALL THROUGH THE NIGHT

Old Welsh Air
Arranged by Nicholl

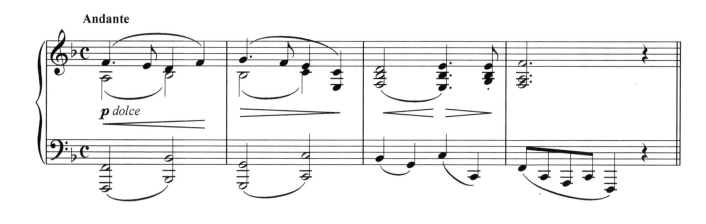

Andante

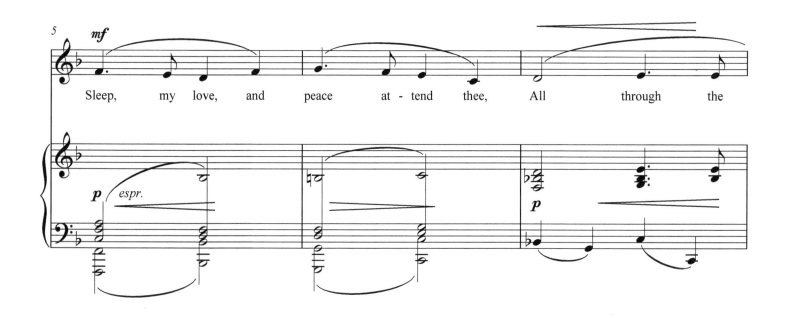

Sleep, my love, and peace at-tend thee, All through the

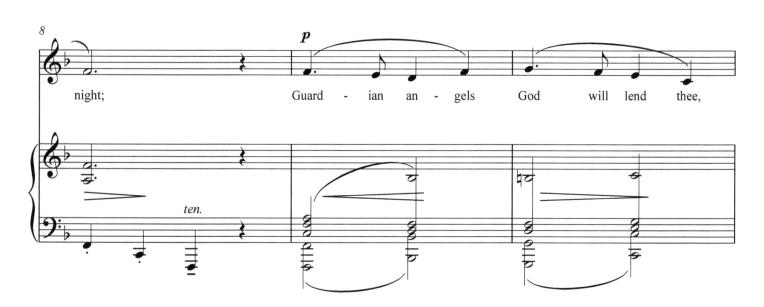

night; Guard - ian an - gels God will lend thee,

All through the night. Soft the drow - sy hours are creep - ing, Hill and vale in slum - ber steep - ing, Love a - lone his watch is keep - ing, All through the night.

CHILDREN'S GAMES

Christian Adolf Overbeck

Wolfgang Amadeus Mozart

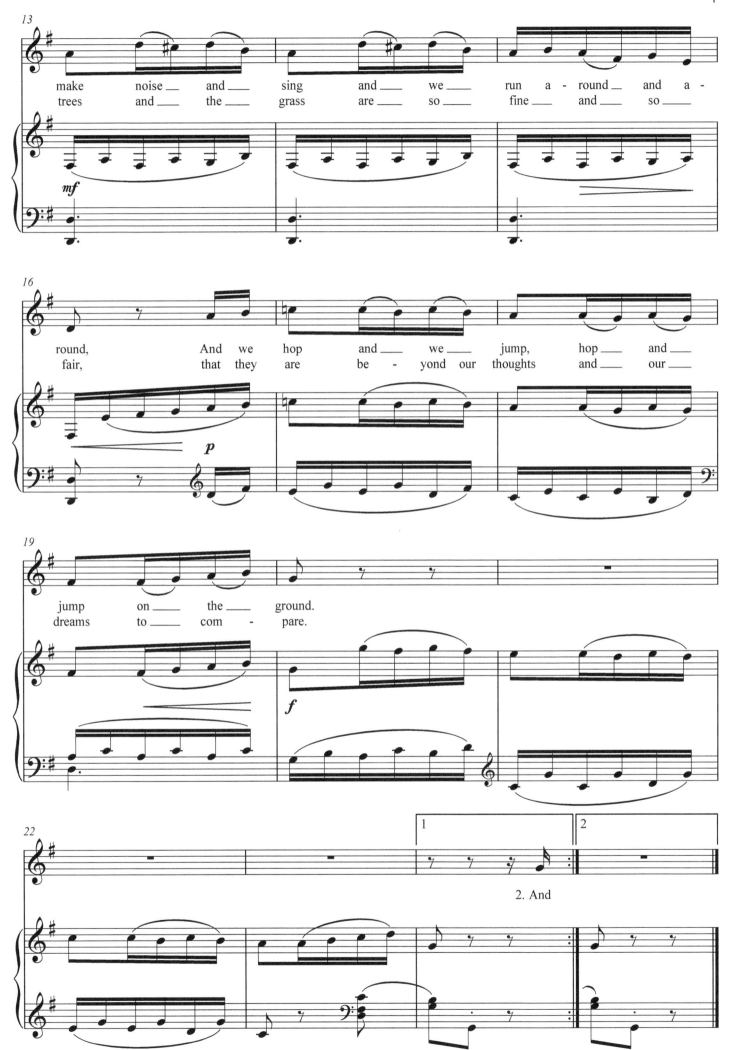

COME TO THE FAIR

Helen Taylor

Easthope Martin

The song has been abbreviated to two verses.

men, To the fair in the pride of the morn -

ing So deck your - selves out in your fin - est ar -

ray, With a heigh - ho! _____

come to the fair! _____

CRADLE SONG

Composer unknown, previously attributed to
Wolfgang Amadeus Mozart

1. Sleep, oh my dar - ling, now
2. Qui - et now reigns in the

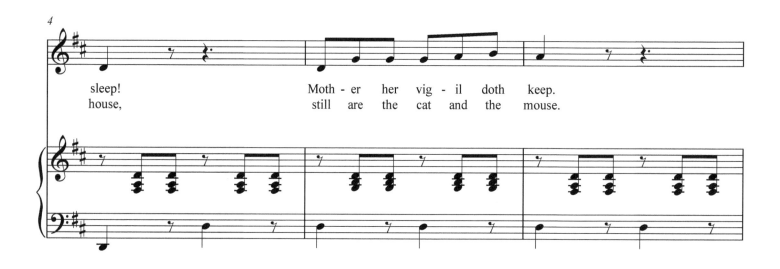

sleep!   Moth - er her vig - il doth keep.
house,   still are the cat and the mouse.

Birds are a - sleep in their nests,   lamb - kins and bees are at rest.
Tur - moil of day now is o'er,   bird - lings are sing - ing no more.

HO! MR. PIPER

Music and Words by
Pearl G. Curran

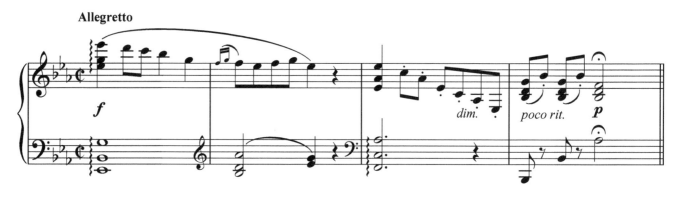

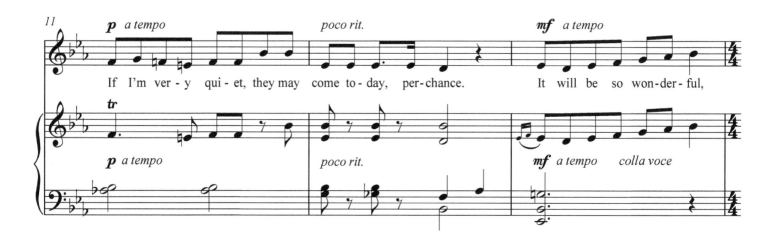

THE LARK IN THE MORN

English Folksong
Collected and arranged by Cecil J. Sharp

Allegretto con grazia

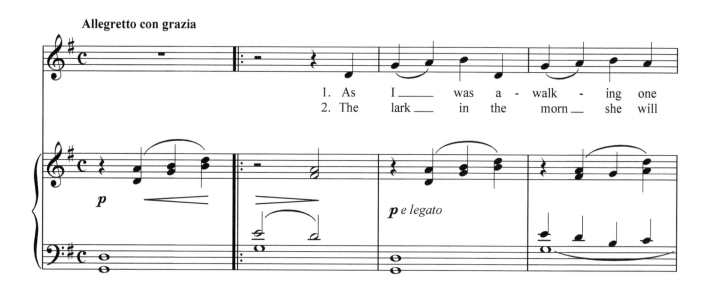

1. As I ___ was a-walk-ing one
2. The lark ___ in the morn ___ she will

morn - ing in the Spring, I met ___ a young
rise up from her nest, And mount ___ in the

dam - sel, so sweet-ly she did sing; And
air ___ with the dew all on her breast; And

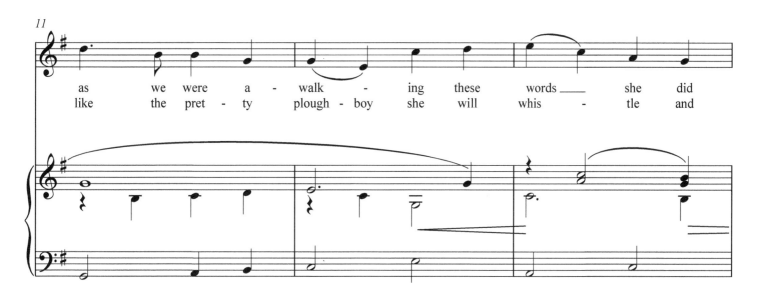

as we were a - walk - ing these words _____ she did
like the pret - ty plough - boy she will whis - tle and

say: _____ There's no life _____ like a plough - boy's all
sing, _____ And at night _____ she'll re - turn _____ to her

cresc.

dim.

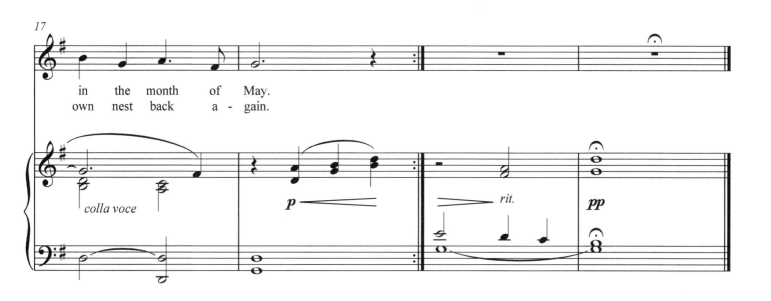

in the month of May.
own nest back a - gain.

colla voce

p

rit.

pp

THE LITTLE SANDMAN

From *Volks-Kinderlieder*
Arranged by Johannes Brahms

LOVE WILL FIND OUT THE WAY

Time of Elizabeth

LULLABY
(Wiegenlied)

English text by Arthur Westbrook

Johannes Brahms

SWINGING

W.K. Clifford

Cécile S. Hartog
Adapted by Joel K. Boyd

This song has been adapted for this edition.

SIMPLE GIFTS

Traditional Shaker Song
Arranged by Richard Walters

THE WATER IS WIDE

Traditional
Arranged by Brendan Fox

A TWILIGHT FANCY
(Dresden China*)

F. E. Weatherley

J. L. Molloy
Adapted by Joel K. Boyd

* Dresden china figurines are a style of porcelain figures from Dresden, Germany.
The song has been adapted for this edition.